Play Church Communion

What, why and how in pictures & play

Collated by Revd C Noppen

Play Church Communion

Copyright 2023 by Chantal Noppen All Rights Reserved

No part of this publication may be reproduced, distributed, or transmitted in any form or by any means, including photocopying, recording, or other electronic or mechanical methods, or by any information storage and retrieval system without the prior written permission of the publisher.

Play Church: Communion

Pastor's preface

This short book is intended to help unpack, explain and direct someone through a simple communion service. It is intentionally word light and picture heavy, with space for notes and doodles. Think pages have pictures to hint at missing words and explain parts of the service. Listen is a bingo page. Learn introduces a bit more detail of some more catholic traditions.

Whether provided as a take-home resource or to use during a service, sensory toys and prayer aids can be used alongside the book to increase the interaction and engagement e.g. squishy globes and hearts, play figures, knitted flowers, water timers, ribbons, memoboards and pens.

The sacrament of communion is central to the Christian faith and really important, let's encourage as many people as possible to want to learn, access and understand why.

God bless

Rev'd Chantal x

Gather

Sorry

Praise

Listen

Pray

Peace

Bless

Break

Eat

Go

GATHER

welcome!
hello

Q: The Lord be with you
A: And also with you!

Think

We take  to collect our  and turn our focus to

Often this is done through 🎵 and

Using a  ⏳ or  may also help

SORRY

Have you **hurt** or **upset** anyone?
Ignored someone?

Not done something you should have?

Be brave, name it!

You might like to write or draw something on a memoboard or some paper you can throw away

LISTEN

Story time!

What can you hear?

Learn

There will usually be at least one Bible reading or story

They will come from the:
Old Testament – before Jesus
New Testament – after Jesus
and the Gospel – during Jesus' life

In some churches the Gospel will be read from the middle of the church, among the people to remind us that it tells us about the time Jesus walked amongst us, on earth as a human.

The readings will be followed by a time of reflection and explanation.

Bible bingo!

Ask	Balance	Bread	Call	City
Cross	Family	Feed	Fish	Fix
Follow	Idea	Money	Music	Peace
Play	Rest	Shop	Storm	Talk
Test	Time	Train	Unlock	Work

Listen out...

PRAY

For **what** and **who** do you pray?

We pray:

 For others

 For ourselves

 For the world

 For creation

 For the sick

 For the dead & those who mourn

Learn

In some traditions bells may be rung during parts of the service.

This is to draw attention to extra *special moments* and actions when the *Holy Spirit* is present and busy.

The bells invite us to *pause* and remind us that communion is about connecting us with God, directly.

The 'Holy Spirit Bus bell' is one way of understanding this practice

Learn

At the end of the service, we are often offered a prayer of blessing before we leave; during this, some people may cross themselves.

Asking God, by touching their head – to be in their thoughts their heart – to inspire their feelings their shoulders, L then R – that they notice God around and amongst their everyday lives

It can be a really simple way of reminding yourself that God isn't just at church, but with you, in you and by you, always. And that our faith is meant for sharing

Go, your mass book has ended...

Play Church Communion

Printed in Great Britain
by Amazon